T0196510

Through the Tears

a Journey Through Grief

Judy S. Joachim

iUniverse, Inc.
New York   Bloomington

Through the Tears
a Journey Through Grief

The views expressed in this work are solely those of the author and do not necessarily reflect the views of the publisher, and the publisher hereby disclaims any responsibility for them.

iUniverse books may be ordered through booksellers or by contacting:

iUniverse
1663 Liberty Drive
Bloomington, IN 47403
www.iuniverse.com
1-800-Authors (1-800-288-4677)

Because of the dynamic nature of the Internet, any Web addresses or links contained in this book may have changed since publication and may no longer be valid.

ISBN: 978-1-4502-5486-1 (sc)
ISBN: 978-1-4502-5487-8 (ebk)

Printed in the United States of America

iUniverse rev. date: 9/13/2010

For my beloved husband Jerry

Preface

I am the richest of women. Not rich by the standard that our society values, such as bank accounts and fancy cars, but by measurement of things more valuable than money. For 36 years I had the pleasure to know, love, admire and be married to the most wonderful person I have ever known; my beloved husband Jerry. His gifts were many and all who knew him or met him were touched by his kindness, his ever present smile, his laughter, his sense of humor, his love of life and all creatures therein. This man never met a stranger, never made an enemy and never caused anyone harm. He was not a millionaire, but his rewards in heaven must be great, for the life he led could reap no less.

I stood on a hill, I prayed to God
My heart filled with anger and sorrow
My shoulders were stiff, my fists were clenched
"Why could he not stay 'til tomorrow"

He was loved by all, gave love in return
Husband, father, brother and son
And countless friends who numbered the stars
And he cared for each and every one

His gifts were many, his faults were few
His smile, his jokes, his laughter
He touched the lives of all he knew
And they loved him ever after

"My child" said God, "You do not see"
"Of his time, do not feel greed"
"His jewels were earned, his crown complete"
"So of this world, there was no longer need"

"You see" God spoke, "Gone to a better place"
"Because he'd known his task since birth"
"His only chore, and his chore fulfilled"
"Was to make life a better place on earth"

I am at fault she cried loudly
Of him, I did not take good care
I always thought there'd be more time
And now his death I can't bear

He always loved me blindly
No judgment, not jealous, never cross
But patience, acceptance and kindness
And I mourn for the love in my loss

Sometimes little things brought me anger
And too busy was I to slow down
Though the things he asked for were simple
And now in my sorrow I drown

No demands was he ever imposing
Yet I did not take time to see
That his life was changing and slipping
But his only concern was for me

Why did God not save you
Why did he not intervene
We spent our lives in worship
And when we needed him, he was nowhere to be seen

What did we do to deserve this
If he could not save you, then who?
Many bad men go on for long lifetimes
Why does "whatever you ask" not ring true?

Why did God not save you
Is it true that God does exist?
It's hard to have faith with heart broken
And my questions will ever persist

Will you take me with you
She cried softly to the man
We've been together many years
Go on...not sure I can

I cannot take you with me
As he whispered his reply
Who'd comfort our dear children
When on their pillows cry

Will you take me with you
Once again she spoke sincere
The children grown and gone their way
No reason leave me here

I cannot take you with me
He replied with tear strewn face
Who would tend my garden
If you left your earthly place

Will you take me with you
Was her plea as twice before
Your garden's fully blossomed
My tending need not more

I cannot take you with me
You have things yet left to do
Who would sing the church psalms
If they did not have you

Will you take me with you
This time her voice showed age
I've lived so long without you
Now time to turn the page

I cannot take you with me
The choice not mine to give
I'm here to give you comfort
And reasons you must live

Will you take me with you
As she breathed her last goodbye
I've done all that you asked me
My time has come to die

I've come to take you with me
I'm waiting at heaven's door
At last I'll take you with me
Where we'll live forever more

I wish I had been with you
When you left this world behind
To hold you hand, to say good-bye
And ease your troubled mind

I wish I had been with you
When you gave up earthly fight
To comfort you and say a prayer
To heaven's gate took flight

I wish I had been with you
Those last moments, they'd be so dear
But I'd beg the Lord, plead for your life
To keep you with us here

For every joy, there is sadness
For every triumph, failure looms
For every light, there is darkness
For every daybreak, nightfall blooms

For every rainbow, clouds will cover
For every flower, weeds will grow
And for every birth, a life is taken
And this the greatest pain you'll know

I cannot face tomorrow
Knowing you will not be there

I cannot face tomorrow
Missing you I cannot bear

I cannot face tomorrow
Pointless my time here on earth

I cannot face tomorrow
My future has no worth

I cannot face tomorrow
To be with you I long to be

I cannot face tomorrow
For the world holds no interest to me

Do you know my heartbreak
Do you know my pain
Did you know his life you took
Brought anguish with no refrain

Do you hear my sobbing
Do you shed a tear
Did you know I'd be so sad
When he was no longer here

Do you try to comfort
Do you grant your peace
Did you know his life meant more
And from life I'd want release

Do you know my heartbreak
Do you know my strife
Did you know his time you took
Would leave a shattered life

I sink deeper into darkness
All consumed by thoughts despair
I can't see the light around me
Though I know it's there somewhere

I sink deeper in the shadows
Knowing joy I'll never see
So I wander onward blindly
Wondering if there's hope for me

I sink deeper into darkness
As I spiral deeper still
Can my life go on without you
Or will my soul with darkness fill

All is quiet, all is nothing
As distraught in heartbreak be
For your death has left me shattered
And all hope is gone from me

They all gathered around you
The day you joined heaven's band
There was Louis in the arms of your mother
And Bibi was holding her hand

And Rodney joined Dallas and Eddie
To give you a tour of this place
Many uncles and aunts gone before you
Came to greet you face to face

Grandparents, friends and neighbors
Gone to heaven many years ago past
Then silently they all stepped aside now
So you could see Jesus as last

With arms open wide he spoke softly
To welcome you and to dry all your tears
And all rejoiced in your presence
And at once you forgot all your fears

And you turned and you glanced down from heaven
And smiled at those you left, because you knew
That their sadness would someday be over
When in heaven they would all be joining you

You always knew
The right thing to do
Our love was true
I depended on you

You always knew
The right words to say
How to brighten my day
What price to pay

You always knew
How to make me smile
To go the extra mile
That laughter was your style

You always knew
God was in your heart
Just where to start
We would never part

Until death.

What's the point of living
When you're lonely, angry, sad
Every day brings painful mem'ries
Missing all the things we had

What's the point of breathing
When so worthless it does seem
If I stop, can I be with you
Because that would be my dream

What's the point of thinking
When my thoughts turn to that day
When your life was taken from me
But I wanted you to stay

What's the point of praying
When unanswered my prayers be
'Cause the only thing I asked for
Was return you home to me

What's the point of living
When you're living without love
So for me there is no living
"Til I'm with you up above

The mysteries of death
No one knows what hide
Do you see your loved ones
Do you know you've died

Do you feel their pain
Do you see their tears
Or are you unaware
Or do you know their fears

Do you watch in silence
Can you give a sign
Do you laugh in heaven
Is all in heaven fine

Do you stand in guard there
Protecting those you love
And are you with your loved ones
Who've already gone above

I wonder do you think of me
In heaven's glory bright
I wonder do you think of me
And cry into the night

I wonder do you miss me
As I miss you every day
I wonder do you miss me
As I do in every way

I wonder do you love me
Though gone, I love you still
I wonder do you love me
And love you I always will

I wonder do you see me
As I see you in all things
I wonder do you see me
For seeing you happiness brings

I'll think of you, miss you, love you
Until together in heaven we'll be
When I'll think of you, love you, see you
For all eternity

No words can compress the sorrow
No words bring hope to tomorrow

No words can contain my emotion
No words can express my devotion

No words take away degradation
No words can describe aggravation

No words can compress the sorrow
As I seek words to get through tomorrow

There is a pain inside me
It will never go away
There is a pain inside me
And I feel it every day

The emptiness I'm knowing
It consumes my every thought
The emptiness I'm knowing
With your precious life was bought

The anger that I'm thinking
Makes it hard to see things clear
For the anger that I'm thinking
Brings me torment, hate and fear

The jealous that I'm hiding
Seems others goes on as before
The jealous that I'm hiding
Seems to break my heart once more

There is a pain inside me
And I know it's always there
There is a pain inside me
And inside me, I can't share

I saw a vision of Jerry
In heaven it took place
He was there with his mom and others I knew
And I saw every one, every face

He was standing in a spot, oh so glorious
And he stopped and he turned to me and spoke
And I listened to his loving words of comfort
And the memories of our life did invoke

In an instant he continued what he was doing
And with closer inspection I could see
Every one gathered here was listening to him
Then the laughter took hold, and was free

I then realized now that Jesus
Standing beside me, was holding my hand
"Ill be with you to guide and to show you the way"
"til rejoined in our heavenly land"

And now through my tears, I found comfort
For our love would continue, as before
And a calm sense of peace embraced me
For I knew I'd be with him ever more

I pray for signs
That there is a God
Protecting, keeping, watching

I pray for dreams
Where I can see you
Talk to you and laugh with you

I pray for answers
To questions of why
Why him, why now

I pray for guidance
For decisions I must make
Without you, alone

I pray for strength
To get through another minute
Another hour, another day

I hear you in my silence
I see you in the night
I feel your arms around me
And I know that it's alright

I smell your shirt worn gently
I taste your favorite pie
And all these things remind me
In earth's cold ground you lie

Though most of these are mem'ries
They seem to happen clear
But all I have are mem'ries
So mem'ries are so dear

I see your face in the clouds in the sky
And I ask the Lord, why you had to die

I hear your voice in the softness of the breeze
And I ask the Lord to guide me so that you I'll always please

I feel your touch in the warmth the sunshines bring
And I ask the Lord for mem'ries and to these I'll always cling

I know you're there, I feel your presence in every way
And I thankful for loving you, every minute of every day

There is no sunshine, only rain
There is no happiness, only pain

There are no rainbows, only gloom
There is no future, all I see is doom

There is no love, for love has died
There is no life, without you by my side

I have tears enough for oceans
Tears enough for oceans three
Tears enough for floods unknowing
My tears no comfort be

I have fears enough for ages
Always fears within my mind
Fears consume my every presence
My fears not left behind

I have sorrow enough for many
Sorrow blinds my waking thought
In my sorrow my life is broken
End to sorrow sought

I am not blind
But I can't see
You walking close
Right next to me

I am not deaf
But I can't hear
You call my name
To calm my fear

I am not mute
But I can't speak
The words I say
All seem so bleak

I am not dead
But not alive
Get through each day
For this I strive

Do they know how much I love him
And have loved him for so long
Every day I weep in silence
Though I try hard to be strong

Do they know how much I miss him
More and more each passing day
It seems the pain is getting stronger
And for solace I do pray

Do they know how much I need him
Need him more than 'ere before
From the moment I awaken
Wonder what life has in store

Do they care that I'm alone now
That's my life without him be
To never see him in this lifetime
Means no joy, I'll ever see

Do they know how much I love him
Know I'd trade his life for mine
Do they know miss him forever
Do they know for him I pine

He was a kind and gentle man
His voice he would never raise
He cared for all, no matter who you were
And of his family, he had nothing but praise

Held children on his knee, Santa to them
And he loved their words and their smiles
And he knew what to say to someone in need
And was supportive in whatever their trials

He touched the lives of many on earth
Family, friends, coworkers, even strangers
Were awed by his goodness, his caring and his love
And he did his best to protect them from dangers

Great love for his family, children, wife and all
And he'd smile at the mention of their name
But in heaven he is gone and he's waiting for us
When we join him, our reward to claim

There is no pain greater
Than that of a broken heart
There is no pain harder
Than my time on earth we're apart

There is no pain stronger
Than losing the one you love
There is no pain deeper
Than wishing to be with you above

There is no pain uncomforted
Than your life quickly taken away
And the pain I know is all these things
And I feel them every day

The wind speaks your name
Rustling through the trees
Whistling through the breeze
Brings me to my knees

The clouds show your face
Glistening in the sky
Gently floating by
With many tears I cry

The rain hears your voice
Washing dust away
Cleansing as it may
I miss you every day

I dreamed you were in heaven
In the beautiful gardens walked
There were flowers of glorious colors
And to many people you talked

Surrounded by beauty majestic
No words can describe the view
And then you began taking pictures
And of course making a joke or two

Then came upon loved ones there before you
Together all met, filled with cheer
And embraced and rejoiced in one another
At the happiness and love all held dear

And then in heaven it grew quiet
As to Jesus all listened as he proclaimed
"It is time to welcome another loved one"
And I listened as he called out my name

You were standing before me in an instant
Your face filled with tears, as was mine
And we knew that together we were now
And as before, our love would still shine

"I've missed you so much, glad to see you"
We spoke to each other as before
And all of heaven was rejoicing
For they knew we were together Forever More

The story of our life
Began the day we met
So much in love we then took vows
"I do" with no regret

Our love grew even stronger
With each and every day
And never did we doubt it
And thankful did we pray

Two children from this union
As blessed as we could be
And through the years continued
To know love constantly

And then one day it happened
You left for heaven's shore
And I am broken hearted
Together on earth no more

But our story does not end here
For our love continues true
We will meet again in heaven
When my time on earth is through

Standing on the patio
I looked into the yard
I saw you, heard you, felt you
And the pain took me off guard

Standing on the patio
I looked into the sky
The birds were chirping, singing
And the mem'ries made me cry

Standing on the patio
I fell on bended knee
To ask the Lord to keep you safe
Until your face I see

If God gave me the choice today
Between to live or die
No hesitation would I have
Be with you not deny

If God gave me the choice today
For me to take your place
I wouldn't even think at all
I'd leave your arms embrace

If God gave me the choice today
Choose any man on earth
I'd choose you each and every time
No one to me more worth

If God gave me a choice today
To choose a different life
No choices would be different
I'd still choose to be your wife

I miss you so much it hurts
Each day a little more
There are times it seems I cannot breathe
And I long for you to walk through the door

I miss you so much it hurts
So hard to believe you're not here
Life doesn't seem to hold much promise
And I hate I must live with the fear

I miss you so much it hurts
In every way possible it seems
The pain in my heart seems to overwhelm
When you died so did all of my dreams

I miss you so much it hurts
I'll hurt 'til the day that I die
My life without you seems hopeless and cold
And to the end of my time I'll ask why

We were as close
As close can be
I needed you
You needed me

Our lives as two
Became as one
We never knew
How soon be done

Our plans cut short
With no fore warn
Who knew that day
You'd not see morn

And so I miss
You more each day
"cause death did steal
Our life away

There is life
There is death
Things that change
In just one breath

There is hate
There is love
There is hope
Sent from above

There is me
There is you
There is knowing
Love is true

There is joy
There is pain
From life's troubles
No refrain

There's beginning
There is end
Escape from death
You can't defend

A star shined bright in winter sky
A newly formed star birth
On eve of New Year this star was formed
And now it shined down on earth

An angel looked down from his heavenly place
And asked the father near
"Where did that new star come from"
"It's light so bright and clear"

"You see" said he "when souls are passed"
"From their life to unknowing"
"Old stars are reborn, but first shine dim"
"But this star's light was glowing"

"It means he was the best of men"
"He was good and loving and kind"
"This star is meant to guide the path"
"Of those he left behind"

"I used this same star a long time ago"
"Before on earth this man born"
"To lead 3 men to proclaim the birth"
"Of my son on Christmas morn"

"And fashioned after Jesus' life"
"This man returned on high"
"And now he's there for all to see"
"As the brightest star in the sky"

As I lay on my bed through pangs of sorrow
A voice spoke to me oh so clear
"I know that it seems you're alone in the world"
"But always know I am here"

"I was there on your birth on that October day"
"I was there on that day when you wed"
"I was there when your children came into the world"
"And I was there when your beloved lay dead"

"And now that he's gone to his heavenly home"
"And you cry and your thoughts so forlorn"
I am there by your side, I am with you always"
"I am there to give comfort as you mourn"

"All you need do is ask, shall receive in return"
"And I promise someday understand"
"Though I know you don't see, through your sorrow and pain"
"But beside you I am holding your hand"

"He is with me in heaven, someday you'll be too"
"So until then take care and be still"
"And know I am God and that my will be done"
"So your destiny you must live to fulfill"

I hate the word widow
I hate the thing it means
I hate the stares you get when said
I hate the outcast scenes

I hate the word widow
I hate the cold, harsh stab
I hate the pain each time I hear
I hate the heart felt jab

I hate the word widow
For it means you've gone far away
I hate the word widow
But a widow I am today

Our plans we'll never realize
Our dreams I now must compromise
My emotions I work to stabilize
While my thoughts and prayers I exercise

Because so few can sympathize
My pain some seem to minimize
From family I feel ostracize
While life I want to penalize

You promised you'd never leave me
But your word you did not keep
You left me here so all alone
And now for you I weep

You promised we'd be together
But your words they were not true
And everyday I face the fact
I must go on without you

You promised to always take care of me
But your words they were a lie
And all day long I hurt so bad
And all I do is cry

But I can't blame you for promises broken
The words you said were true in your heart
You didn't know God's intentions
That from earth too soon you'd depart

For my wife I'm praying
That peace will come your way
I know my death unplanned for
And you will miss me every day

But life goes on, believe that
And you must go on, for me
Nothing has changed between us
I'm just not there that you see

Pick up your gloomy thoughts now
A smile on your face you must find
And know that I'll always love you
Even though I have left you behind

"God has a plan for you"
I keep hearing people say
But what kind of plan could include
Missing you so much each day

There could be no plan for me
That would include living without you
And if there is, I can't accept
'cause our dreams cannot come true

I've no interest in life without you
It holds no future I anticipate
So I don't seek a plan for my future
Because my loss for my love is too great

Through my tears, which clouds my head
I begged for mercy, take my life instead
His life oh so perfect, a man of good deeds
A man concerned for other people's needs

His humor unmatched, his smile ever present
His kindness extreme, his manner always pleasant
And though I am still living, in heaven he will be
But someday I will see him, when God chooses me

The pain in my heart overwhelming
Just to breathe, I struggle for air
I wake in the night for a glimpse of your face
And I remember you are no longer there

My mind is flooded with memories
Of the great times we had in the past
I dream of a future, the plans we had made
And the emptiness grows and is vast

I pray every moment to see you
For one more brief moment to say
I will love you forever 'til my time is come
Then in heaven I'll join you that day

The world seems to go on without you
A fact that is hard to comprehend
It seems it should stop just as you did
And for me to go on, I pretend

People around me, their lives keep on moving
While my life seemed to end on that day
I don't want to face another tomorrow
And I can't find the will just to pray

So don't talk of future when mine ended
And I don't want to hear of your joy
All left for me is my mem'ries
Of this girl and that very special boy

The mention of your name brings sorrow
The mention of your name brings joy
And the love that is still between us
Even death's grip cannot destroy

Your picture on the wall brings sadness
Your picture on the wall brings a smile
And I'm thankful for our wonderful time together
Even though it was too short a while

Your hand on my shoulder brings me comfort
Your hand on my shoulder guides my way
Though your body no longer beside me
I feel your presence every day

There can be no more happiness
Since you left me here behind
There can be no more contentment
To that I am resigned

There can be no more laughter
No more laughter will I know
There can be no more trusting
Always fearful where I go

There can be no more patience
For my patience wearing thin
There can be no more fulfillment
Disappointment closes in

Matters not if years I'm given
Or if today my last day be
I can never again know comfort
That your love provided me

"Jerry please don't leave me"
Are the words I would have said
If I had the chance been given
As you lay upon death's bed

"I can't live without you"
I'd have pleaded in your ear
But no chance was I given
To try and keep you here

"Jerry take me with you"
Would it work, no one can say
'cause no chance was I given
To beg you here to stay

He was a man so special
He lived his life as one should
He loved his wife and family
Did good deeds whenever he could

He never judged worth by money
He cared more for integrity and respect
Never tried to give false impressions
And never met a person he'd reject

He always saw a problem as opportunity
To turn things around for the best
And those whom he led were astonished
That he was always calm, never stressed

In everyone he met he found goodness
And he lived and loved life more than most
He was honest and caring, always joyful
Of his accomplishments he never would boast

So when I say he was special, believe me
From the moment he was born, until the end
And he lives in our memories forever
Though our broken hearts never will mend

In all the world
There seems to be
No love or laughter
Left in me

In all the world
I cannot feel
The pain so deep
It cannot heal

In all the world
It seems so much
I long and yearn
For your soft touch

In all the world
Search high and low
Why am I here
Why did you go

In all the world
There seems to be
No greater love
Than you and me

In my dreams we are together
We are standing hand in hand
While the ocean sprays our faces
And our toes sink in the sand

In my dreams we are together
We are sitting face to face
In a garden full of beauty
Listening to the quiet space

In my dreams we are together
We are walking arm in arm
Watching day turn into sunset
From life's troubles feel no harm

In my dreams we are together
We are sleeping side by side
Though in earth we both are placed now
And on heaven's shore, reside

When I get to heaven
Your face again I'll see
Your smile, your nose, your twinkling eyes
A joyful time will be

When I get to heaven
Your voice I'll finally hear
Your stories, laughter, good advice
Bring pleasures to my ear

When I get to heaven
Your hand I'll hold again
A walk along the grassy hill
Will be our daily plan

When I get to heaven
If so granted by the Lord
We'll spend our days together
In our heavenly reward

Life is short
Those words be true
For death comes quick
As did to you

Life is pain
That much I know
I feel it deep
I feel it grow

Life is guilt
For things done wrong
And for repair
We always long

Life is death
No one escape
And of that truth
We can't debate

I'm mad at you for leaving
No warning, no goodbye
Just up and gone with no response
And everyday I cry

I'm mad at your not listening
Your health, tried to express
Take better care, who knows the cost
But mostly you thought less

I'm mad at you for leaving
Now all alone am I
So many years without you
To think and ponder why

Through my tears, I heard your voice
Telling me, have strength and go on
I know you are sad and I am sad too
"cause together on earth our time gone

But our love transcends so together we'll be
Always, when you reach heaven's shore
So hold on until then though time may seem long
But hand in hand we'll be once more

No blame should you feel, no control did you have
Of God's plan, which is not yet revealed
And though you don't understand and your pain is so deep
Together again, and your heart will be healed

So cherish the memories and many great times we had
And those memories will carry you through
'cause you know that I love you, 'til the end of all time
And I'm waiting in heaven for you

The light in your eyes extinguished
The light in your heart ever shows
The strength in your limbs abandoned
The strength in your soul still grows
The warmth in your body turned cold now
The warmth in your smile never cease
The touch of your hand gone forever
The touch of your life brings us peace

I am lost
Just as when the lights have been extinguished in an unfamiliar place
And I cannot find my way

I am alone
As if the entire human race has ceased to exist
And I am left abandoned in a cold, dark, world

I am sad
As if the joy of my heart has been drowned in tears
That cannot be consoled

I am no more
For the person I was is not the same
The future I anticipated will never be
And the happiness of my life has been silenced

I wait by the window to see you
Then realize you are no longer there
I listen for your voice just to hear you
And I remember no sound anywhere

I look in the garden to find you
But though look as I might…you're not found
I reach for your touch in the darkness
Though I know you're no longer around

I think of the mem'ries so dear now
Of a man that I loved and love still
And I know he is right here beside me
And I know in my heart, always will

No one could love me like you did
No one else could know my ways
You were always there to support me
You always brought joy to my days

Arguments were nary between us
You were always considerate and kind
You always knew my talents
Of my faults you were forgiving, not blind

No one could love me like you did
And you did love me, that I know true
No one could love me like you did
And I could love no one but you

I know your heart was broken
When you left me here behind
Your love for me beyond compare
For me brought peace of mind

I know you cried as I did
When together we'd no longer be
For separated by death too soon
And my face you'd no longer see

I know you dreamed as I did
Of a future no longer in store
So I pray that together soon we will be
United on heaven's shore

Those brown eyes filled with laughter
Brought joys to many far and wide
Your humor and wit so delightful
Made it easy to stand by your side

Never a frown or harsh word did you utter
It was not in your nature to cause hurt
For your kindness and patience always present
And never words of anger did you blurt

So in heaven they requested your presence
For they needed another angel good and true
And the Lord he is smiling in his glory
For he knows few can measure up to you

They say time heals
I've heard it many times
But is time some medicine
That from darkness sunshine climbs

Time cannot be friendly
'cause in time I might forget
Your voice, your smile, your face, your walk
And that my worst pain yet

Pain, Anguish, Loneliness, Sorrow
I live these today, I'll live these tomorrow
Shock, Frustration, Anger, Devastation
Trade my life for his, without hesitation
Yesterday, Today, Tomorrow, Forever
I'll always love you and forget you never

To my wife, I love you
Our years together the best
Know that I miss you each moment
Know that my life was so blessed

I ache for the pain my death has caused you
And it hurts me to see you this way
So I asked our Lord to show mercy
And give you needed strength today

My wife, I'll love you forever
And I ask that you go on as best you can
And know that this all has a purpose
For it is all part of God's special plan

To my wife, I'm waiting
By the pearly gates I'll wait every day
Until you time here is ended
Then together in heaven we will stay

No one can stop the pain
Of my heart's shattered pieces
No one can stop the hurt
As my loss each day increases
No one can stop the tears
As the mem'ries flood my mind
No one can stop the emptiness
As I've been left behind
No one can stop the guilt
Of the way things might have been
And all I have to hold onto
Is someday together again

This is the year I call the "firsts"
Difficult in every way
Each holiday or special occasion
Without you, despise the day

First Valentine's, Anniversary, Thanksgiving
Each one no easy time
Even the first trip on a Sunday to church
Was not eased by thoughts sublime

I think of our first year together
And more precious than all jewels combined
Are my mem'ries of love shared completely
A love that no boundaries defined

Did you know you were dying
Did you know, did you know
As on the bed were lying
Did you know, did you know

Did you hear the angels beckon
Did you hear, did you hear
As your life they came to reckon
Did you hear, did you hear

Did you feel my heart was breaking
Did you feel, did you feel
As you last breath were taking
Did you feel, did you feel

Did you know you were dying
Did you know, did you know

I never had to worry
I had never had much fear
I never had to think about
Which way I'd go from here

I went through life not wondering
Who'd see me through each day
I knew you'd always be there
I knew it would be OK

But that is not the same now
I worry the whole day through
How do I make right choices
When before relied on you

Our lives so intertwined then
Our decisions we made as one
So I'm lost and all alone now
But from life I cannot run

For every joy you encounter
Someone's soul is filled with sorrow
For every success you are awarded
Another has trouble facing tomorrow

For every friend you sat and talked with
There is someone who is lonely
For every marriage vows are taken
Someone has lost their one and only

For every song you hear for dancing
There is someone who hears silence
For every life filled up with love
Someone's life is filled with violence

For every sunrise you awaken
For every dusk you live to see
Remember those whose life's misfortunes
Need your prayers on bended knee

I dreamed we were together
Our faces showed years of life
We sat on a bench, we were hand in hand
Together as husband and wife

We talked, we laughed, we told stories
Of days gone by through the years
And we'd stop just to watch and to listen
There was no sorrow, no sadness, or tears

We sat there for hours unending
"til the sunset peaked o'er the shore
And was followed by dark all around me
And we were sitting together no more

I awoke and mem'ry regained now
Of another sunset we never would see
And I'll see other sunsets without you
But our next sunset in heaven will be

There is no joy
There is only pain
There is no sunshine
There is only rain

There are no flowers
All replaced by weeds
There is no music
Only noise an instrument bleeds

There is no beauty
Only ugly rears its head
For I am living
And my beloved is dead

You say there is a God
But proof of this I need
For if he had almighty power
Then why does my heart bleed

He could have chose to save him
Instead of standing by
So why would God with such power
Leave me asking why

You say there is a God
Well if I meet him face to face
I'll tell him the anger and pain that he left
And the hole in my heart, no replace

And everyday I question
His death, if a loving God there be
He should have saved my husband
From death's grip been set free

At the pearly gates, his name was read
Though years too soon, from this life he was led
His book of deeds was raised for judge
Too heavy to lift, too heavy to budge

When in a loud voice God himself did tell
"I know this man clearly, and I know this man well"
"A good life he lived, nary an unkind thing done"
"His life an example to each and everyone"

"I called him home early, and I called him with no haste"
"Many loved ones left behind, his life was not a waste"
"He was one of my angels, sent down from above"
"To fill those he met with happiness and fill those he met with love"

"Though his time seemed short, by measure of earthly years"
"He brought joy, laughter, kindness and his departure many tears"
"His life will be long and joyful though they do no see"
"For in heaven he will live…for all eternity"

Will you know me when I get there
If it's many years from now
You'll be young and still so handsome
I'll be old and wonder how

You'll still run and walk so quickly
I'll be slow and walk with cane
You'll still hear the birds singing
But for me their song in vain

You'll still see much like an eagle
I'll not see the things you see
Will you know me when I get there
Will you know that it is me

You are gone
And I am left here
Crying, missing you, wishing to be with you

You are gone
And the once beautiful world in which we lived
Is now cold, dark and lonely

You are gone
And all the love in my heart went with you
And I can no longer see past the shattered pieces

You are gone
And I shall forever hold your memory in my heart
I shall forever miss you
And I shall forever love you

Another sign you sent to me
As plain as plain can be
A bird so lovely, we had hoped
Together we would see

He flew into a favorite bush
And sat so still and waited
Until was sure he caught my eye
As sunlight's rays had faded

He flew right by and perched again
Ever closer that before
And I knew 'twas you the instant I saw
A sign I could not ignore

And as a smile came to my face
As quick as he came, he took flight
To the heavens he flew, having sent there by you
And I watched as the day turned to night

How can I recall
That wretched, horrid day
When life changed so abruptly
And took your love away

How can I remember
That cold and wintry morn
We laid to rest your body
From our loving arms were torn

How can I consider
What your death has done to me
My broken heart reminds me
I must live in misery

How can I keep living
When my heart knows love no more
And I pray that you'll be waiting
When I get to heaven's shore

Arms outstretched before him
Blinded by the light
Pulled away from all he knew
Resisted though he might

Hands reached out to gently
Escort him on his way
Jesus and countless angels
No words to him did say

He tried in vain to get back
To those he left behind
A wife and sons and many more
Engulfed his weary mind

Then the realization
That life was his no more
Then Jesus spoke right to him
As they walked through heaven's door

And suddenly all grew quiet
As earth's pull had no hold
And all in heaven rejoicing
And welcomed him to heaven's fold

Though his time on earth long gone now
He thinks of those he'll always love
And he watches and protects them every moment
From his heavenly home up above

Those that know cry with me
"You will never get over his death"
"You simply learn to live with the pain"
"And just learn to take your next breath"

Those with experience say to me
"You'll miss him every minute of every day"
"You just learn how to move forward"
"And everyday you pray"

Those that know cry with me
For they know the pain we endure
The loved ones we are missing
Leaves a heartache from which there's no cure

Would I choose to marry
If I'd known would end so soon
If I had known the song of pain
Would I choose a different tune

Would I choose to love you
If I'd known you'd not have stayed
'cause our duet a solo
Our music now is played

Would I choose a lifetime
Of being on my own
If I could see your time so short
Would I choose it if I'd known

Would I choose to marry
Well the simple truth is clear
I'd choose our life together
And I'd choose it without fear

A couple of kids when we met
Best friends almost instantly
A lifetime of love we shared
Unbreakable bond were we

We planned a lifetime together
Not knowing it would all end so soon
But a lifetime of love we were blessed with
Now my heart sings a heartbroken tune

We were lucky to have found each other
It was fate from beginning, meant to be
And though we're apart for this lifetime
I will hold your love close here with me

There are many that say
"I know how you must feel"
But unless you've lost the one you love
To you I must appeal

Your words do not bring comfort
In fact they bring me pain
I understand you mean no harm
But from those words please refrain

So listen when I tell you
Speak only what you know
Of sadness, love or great memories
Or your heart felt grief bestow

For in your darkest hour
Someday you'll understand
How words though unintended
Can sting like the slap of a hand

There is nary a minute I don't think of you
And few when tears are not shed
The mem'ries of you and the love that we shared
Constantly flood through my head

Disbelief is still strong, in shock still am I
For too young and untimely your leaving
And I pray and I hope to see you again soon
Until then, all is suffering and grieving

No sunshine I've seen, nor blue skies above
The world is dark and cold and unfeeling
And I know if you could, you'd be here by my side
And together in prayer we'd be kneeling

The warmth of your love, from heaven to earth
And I feel it so strong and so true
Though distance separates the people we were
Please know, I will always love you

I know you are beside me
As I carry on my day
To watch me and to keep me safe
And help me find my way

I feel your presence always
Whether morning, noon or night
And I wish that I could see you
And I wish with all my might

I know you'll never leave me
Inside my heart you'll be
And I love you more than ever
And I'm thankful you loved me

I know you are beside me
Ever present ever strong
And someday both in heaven
Together we belong

Do people think I've forgotten
If I smile, or laugh, or joke
But they can't see what's hidden
In my heart forever broke

Do people think disgraceful
If I go to work each day
And try to live a normal life
In my own painful way

Do people think I don't love you
If they don't see me cry
I do the best to hide my tears
So they don't ask me why

Do people think they know me
Or they know how I must feel
But if they could see inside me
They'd see wounds that cannot heal

Memories wash over me
Like Niagara rushing fast
Each one knocking the breath out
Each one part of our past

All memories are so precious
They tell the story true
Of a man both loved and loving
Of my memories of you

Wonderful memories yet painful
Each one is bittersweet
Yet I'm desperate for the memories
Without them, incomplete

Anger and fear cloud my mind
I'm unable to see past this grief
Shut off from the world in darkness I dwell
And I hope my time left is brief

A world without you, not a good place
And I long for your smile and your touch
And though others may plead me move forward
I can't when I miss you so much

Anger and sorrow cloud my mind
Overwhelmed with grief and despair
A pain from which no one can release me
A pain that will always be there

I searched for you in silence
But no words did I receive
I searched for you in raindrops
But the dampness caused me leave

I searched for you in sunshine
But it only burned my face
I searched for you in darkness
But in darkness lost my place

I searched for you in heaven
Where the angels song resound
'Search no more, he is here with us"
So in heaven you were found

I feel you in the silence
I feel you in the rain
I feel you in the air I breathe
I feel you in my pain

I see you in the flowers
I see you in the trees
I see you in the grass that grows
I see you in the breeze

I hear you in the ocean
I hear you in the wind
I hear you in the birds that sing
I'll hear you 'til my end

Save me a place in heaven
Next to you a spot
I'll be there as soon as my life is through
However much time I've got

Build us a house in heaven
Big enough for all our kin
As large as can be with flowers and trees
And filled with happiness within

I'll soon join you in heaven
Together once more we'll know love
'til the end of all time our love will shine
In our beautiful mansion above

God put you on earth
Part of a family like no other
Your love for both your parents
And every sister and brother

God put you on earth
To bring happiness to your wife
For many great years together
You made a wonderful life

God put you on earth
To help guide your children's way
Your daily care and devotion
They received from you each day

God put you on earth
To be a leader in work place
Your integrity and kindness
Always a smile for every face

God put you on earth
Though too short your time would be
And each of us will count the days
Your face again we'll see

He was more than just my husband
Was my soulmate, my best friend
From the time when we first dated
All our time together'd spend

He always stood beside me
I was at his side as well
We crossed life's roads together
Both as one we never fell

He was oh so close to perfect
Not a bad word could I say
Always making people happy
That was just his kindly way

Always thoughtful of all creatures
Whether bird or dog or man
Never causing an injustice
Always strived to live God's plan

Now he's gone back up to heaven
God must need him for some chore
But I shall miss him every minute
'til I knock in heaven's door

In my darkest hour
I long to be by your side
In the cold, dark, earth
Untouched by the warmth of the sunlight

In my darkest hour
I cannot forgive myself for those lost, stolen moments
No chance to say "I love you"
Say goodbye
Or hold your hand

In my darkest hour
I curse a God who could so easily rip you from this life
And leave behind a heart that is broken and shattered
While only a shell remains

And in my darkest hour
I see no joy, no comfort. no solace, only pain and eternal sorrow
For my life has no meaning
In a world without you

Today is our anniversary, my love
Though not here, you remain in my heart
I found it so hard to get through the day
And I prayed from this world to depart

No greater love could two people share
Though no last moments I have to remember
And I cry and I weep as I think on that day
When you were taken that last day in December

And I'm grateful for years of much happiness had we
A lifetime of love we were blessed
Though numbered on earth, too short our time spent
But forever in eternal rest

So Happy Anniversary my love, the best years of my life
So you've gone our heavenly home to prepare
But I'll see you again soon, only God will know when
And only then will my heart see repair

The face I see in the mirror
Gazing back as I look in its stare
Is not the face I remember
And I don't recognize the person there

The face I see in the mirror
Is forever changed, forever blank, forever lost
The expressions once lit with happiness
Are replaced by your death's heavy cost

The face I see in the mirror
Is a reflection of sorrow that will never cease
But someday the face in the mirror
When beside you will at last know peace

There are none beside me
On this lonely path I tread
There are none beside me
As the anger fills my head

There are none beside me
As I search for you in vain
There are none beside me
As my heart is filled with pain

There are none beside me
As the men'ries flood my mind
There are none beside me
"cause you left me here behind

There are none beside me
From the morning through the night
There are none beside me
Wish for strength with all my might

There are none beside me
Though it seems from day to day
But the one who is beside me
Whispers to me as I pray

No one cares
No one tries
To see the pain
Behind my eyes

The tears I shed
Each day and night
To wish someone
Could make it right

I'd choose to go
If had my way
To stand beside you
There today

Can't say goodbye
So live in hell
But death will come
Though when not tell

His smile…could melt a heart of ice
His laughter…such joy he could entice
His kindness…could save a person from despair
His thoughtfulness…there were few who could compare
I loved him…and he loved me in return
I miss him…but live without him I must learn

Don't talk to me of happy times
With your husband, family or wife
'cause these are things that hurt so much
And 'cause pain to my life

Don't tell me of your future plans
Vacations, retirement and such
'cause these are things we'll never know
And it makes me miss him much

Don't tell me of your perfect life
No idea the sorrow it brings
'cause our happy times and future no more
To hear yours, my heart it stings

I can't control the tears
That so freely drench my face
And wash away the make-up
So carefully put in place

I can't control my thoughts
Of that last fateful day
Things I wish done different
Things wished I could say

I can't control my hatred
For those that let you die
And through my tears and anguish
My anger I can't deny

I can't control my heartbreak
I can't control my pain
I can't control the loneliness
From emotions I can't abstain

He was the perfect husband
Always loving, always kind
Always generous and supportive
The best in all the world you'd find

He was the perfect father
Never raised his voice, was fair
He filled the house with laughter
When they needed him, was there

He was the perfect brother
Pride for each always displayed
Never criticized or angered
Time for each he always made

He was the perfect son
For he loved his parents so
Now he's with his mom in heaven
And her love again he'll know

The end of your life came too sudden
The end of my life yet to see
The end of our time on earth over
The end of our love will never be

The end of each day brings the darkness
The end of a book words must cease
The end of a year, expectations
The end of the tears, hope for peace

The end so final, so forever
The end is completion, no time left
The end cannot change words unspoken
The end leaves us lonely and bereft

The end is also the beginning
The end of heartbreak and pain we know
For the end brings us to the arms of Jesus
And in the end to heaven we hope to go